WARNING:
This book will make you more creative!

Includes 425 Heartwarmin'
(and humorous) Expressions.
Use to decorate personal
and unique gifts, greetings,
memory albums,
seasonal and home decor
craft projects.

Spread
Some
Smiles

Crafty Secrets Publications

ISBN 0-9699410-4-8

9 780969 941040

W6-BSM-161

425 Heartwarmin' Expressions

A Workbook for Crafting, Painting or Stitching

by Sandy Redburn & Shelly Ehbrecht

Crafty Secrets Publications
15430 78A Ave.
Surrey, B.C. Canada
V3S 8R4

Copyright © 1995, Revised 1997 Sandy Redburn. Crafty Secrets Publications.
All rights reserved. With purchase of this book you have permission to trace, photocopy and enlarge the expressions, graphics or alphabets to aid you in the application onto your projects, for personal fun or crafting profit. However, if you are mass producing (100+) items with our expressions, please request permission. No part of this book may be reproduced for any other means under federal copyright laws, except by a reviewer who may quote brief excerpts.

Disclaimer: The information in this book has been brought to you in good faith. We have no control over the physical conditions surrounding the application of the information presented. We disclaim any liability.

ISBN 0-9699410-4-8

Table of Contents

Category Themes

• •

There is a smorgasbord of creative supplies and helpful aids for lettering expressions
onto an almost endless array of surfaces. Check with your local retail stores for products
from the manufacturers listed below.

Permanent Markers
EK Success
(Zig Markers)
611 Industrial Rd.
Carlstadt, NJ 07072-6507
Phone (201) 939-5404
Fax   (201) 939-4511

Permanent Markers
Sakura of America
(Pigma® Ink Products)
30780 San Clemente St.
Hayward, CA 94544-7131
Phone (510) 475-8880
Fax   (510) 475-0973

Needle Craft Alphabets
ASN Publishing
1455 Linda Vista Drive
San Marcos, CA 92069
Phone (760) 471-2320
Fax   (760) 591-0230

Walnut Hollow Farm. Inc.
1409 State Road 23
Dodgeville, WI
53533-2112
Phone (608) 935-2341
Fax   (608) 935-3029

Introduction

Expressions and phrases have been shared, enjoyed and passed down for centuries around the world. They usually contain some form of values, inspiration or humor. Some become national proverbs. Phrases such as "Home Sweet Home", "God is Love" and "Practice Makes Perfect" are common internationally.

Given the complex, often stressful lives we lead today, it's no surprise people are searching for ways to regain more of the simple pleasures life can hold. Studies show we have become more focused on our spirituality, values, family traditions, friendships, homes, hobbies and health. Adding heartwarmin', inspirational and humorous expressions to gifts, greetings, clothing, seasonal and home decor crafts and keepsakes has become a popular trend. How wonderful, we have something in style that offers unlimited creative possibilities for creating some warm fuzzies and smiles both in our lives and those of others.

From the beginning, our goal was to create a fun, heartwarmin' workbook that could be used for a wide variety of craft and hobby interests, skills and mediums. Those with limited creative skills and budgets can relax. You don't need a lot of talent or money to put this book into action. The craft and sewing industry is overflowing with innovative and easy to use supplies, simplified techniques and aids. By using

a paintbrush, pen and ink, or needle and thread, you can apply these expressions to give a more personal and unique touch to all kinds of creative projects. Look around you for possibilities. You likely already have some bare surfaces waiting to be transformed into a sentimental family treasure, or a whimsical feel good statement.

We want these pages to warm your heart, tickle your funny bone and inspire you to create. We also hope you will remember to pull this book out when; you are faced with a blank card and can't think of anything to write, when you want to add a personal touch to a gift, if you have a child looking for a rainy day craft project, or when you need to just sit back and have a smile.

We enjoyed brainstorming and compiling each chapter so much, we even joked around about introducing a line of "Heartwarmin' Expressions Wallpaper". Plaid Enterprises now manufactures blank wall border paper so you can create your own!

A heartwarmin' thanks to YOU for buying our book. Have great fun spreading smiles!

Sandy & Shelly

Shelly has received her CDD, (Certified Demonstrators Diploma) and enjoys teaching folk art painting and creative lettering classes. She is also a registered nurse on a maternity ward and lives a happy, busy life with her husband and two daughters

Sandy's dedication to inspiring others' creativity includes teaching seminars, writing and publishing books since 1993, including "Crafty Marketing - Jumpstart Your Craft Business". She runs her successful homebased business with the help of her other passion, her husband and three daughters.

Easy Lettering Tips & Tricks

Lettering is not as hard as you may think and, as you will see throughout this book, by no means does it have to be perfect or for that matter straight! You can do your lettering by free hand, or you can trace our expressions and designs right onto your project.

If you would like your lettering larger, you can recreate any expression using the enlarged alphabets in the back of this book. You may also photocopy any expressions and have them enlarged or reduced to fit your personal needs.

Trace or pencil on your lettering first, to get your spacing right. A good eraser and see-through plastic ruler are two very helpful tools for lettering.

It's Easy!

1. Use a pencil & ruler. Lettering does not have to be even - just consistent.
2. Hold pens in an upright position.
3. When possible pull your pen rather than push.
4. Add extra embellishments to create different styles.
5. Get bravely creative - but remember practice and patience.

Dot lettering seems to be the most popular and easiest style of printing to reproduce. Remember you do not have to embellish your letters with dots. As you will see, you can change your printing style by adding hearts, stars, flowers, snowflakes, holly, stitching lines and more!

There are countless design books available, with wonderful patterns to which you can trace and add expressions. Look around you for inspiration and designs that you can match with expressions. Once you start, you will find life offers endless "perfect spots" to add a Heartwarmin' Expression or tickle some funny bones.

Country   Stitchin'

Home or Home

Inspiration or Inspiration

Gardening or Gardening

expression

Family

Put your heart in it

Using Pens & Markers

Using Pens and markers is easy and fun because they are now available in a multitude of tip styles, sizes and colors in both water based and permanent inks. Water based pens work well for a variety of paper crafts, but permanent pigma ink markers won't fade and can be used on a large variety of surfaces. The manufacturers of these markers all agree you should hold your pens in an upright position so the tip has full contact with the writing surface. It may feel a bit awkward but will give you the true essence of the pen tip. You will also find you have better control of your pen when you pull it towards you rather than pushing it away.

Our samples below show how different combinations of pen tips can give your lettering loads of personality and style.

Stitchin

Letters - Pigma Graphic 3,
Stitch Lines - Pigma Micron 01

Family

Letters - Pigma Graphic 3, Outline - Zig 08 Millennium,
Stiches & Heart - Pigma Micron 03

Hearts

Letters - Zig 08 Millennium,
Hearts - Pigma Micron 01

Housework Stinks

Letters - Zig 08 Millennium,
Embellishments - Pigma Micron 03

Life

Letters - Zig 08 Millennium,
Shade - Pigma Micron 03

MOM

Letters - Pigma Micron 01,
Dots - Pigma Micron 05

Inspiration

Letters - Sakura Brush Marker
Dots - Pigma Micron 01
Snowflakes - Pigma Micron 03

Creative Possibilities

Transferring expressions and designs is not difficult. You can mix and match expressions with any pattern and design. Once you decide on an expression and image you want to use, lay tracing paper over it and draw it out. Lay your traced design on your project surface and slip some transfer paper in between your design and prepared surface. Trace the outline with a stylus or empty pen tip. Saral® manufactures a Wax-Free Transfer paper that works on paper, wood, fabric, metal, glass, tile, ceramic, etc. Wax free paper will not clog the tips of your markers and pens. Heat activated transfer pencils also work well on fabric.

● ●

Expressions On Wood

There are so many different painting styles, techniques and decorative finishes used on wood today, it can make your head swim. Some popular applications include primitive to fancy overlay stencils, block printing, antiquing, faux finishing, traditional tole painting, pen and ink watercolors, rustic country or folk art painting. You just need to match your design to the right expression and style of lettering.

If you don't have a steady hand for doing your lettering with a paintbrush don't worry, you can cheat and use permanent markers. When you apply dots to letters on wood, use paint rather than your pen tip. Not only will you save the life of your pens, you can create dots faster and more consistent in size using paint. Dots can be made using a brush tip, stylus or embossing tool. We use corsage pins and various plastic headed pins for different size dots. Stick the pins into the eraser tip of a pencil and just dip the head into paint. When using permanent markers for lettering, test any

varnish first. Krylon manufactures sprays and varnishes that won't make the ink in permanent markers bleed.

Walnut Hollow manufactures wood burning pens, which are perfect for adding letters and designs you have traced onto wood. We also love using their oil colored pencils on wood projects, available in 36 rich, vibrant and metallic colors.

Expressions On Paper Crafts

Use expressions to create your own special occasion and seasonal decorations, birthday cards, photo memory albums and scrapbooks, framed calligraphy, greeting cards, gift tags, invitations, stationary and wrapping paper. Jazz up your projects with colored pencils and inks, watercolors, metallic markers, glitter pens, decorative punches and scissors, templates, stencils, stickers, rubber stamps, 3D or traditional decoupage, paper mold reliefs and more!

Painting Expressions On Fabric

First pre-wash fabric to remove any sizing and don't use any fabric softener. You can use a heat activated transfer pencil, or place some fabric transfer paper between your design and fabric (following all manufacturers' directions). Before painting your transferred design, place a piece of cardboard under your fabric surface (a cookie sheet will also work). Use fabric paints or regular acrylics mixed with a textile medium. Look for quality brushes recommended for textile painting, fabric markers, or use the mini tips on paint bottles to do your lettering.

Expressions On Glass & Ceramics

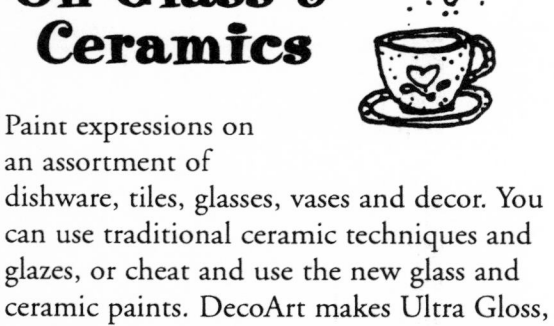

Paint expressions on an assortment of dishware, tiles, glasses, vases and decor. You can use traditional ceramic techniques and glazes, or cheat and use the new glass and ceramic paints. DecoArt makes Ultra Gloss, a paint which becomes permanent when baked in your oven. Delta Perm Enamel is a new air drying permanent paint made for glossy and hard to adhere surfaces.

Expressions By Needle & Thread

Stitching includes an array of techniques for applying expressions, using fancy threads, floss, yarns, ribbons or beads. Machine or hand embroidery, hand stitching on felt, needlepoint, cross stitch, plastic canvas, quilted appliqués and silk ribbon embroidery are all popular decorative embellishments. You can stitch expressions on baby bibs to bumper pads, decorative pillows, wall samplers, aprons, linens, sweatshirts, vests, jumpers, jean jackets, boxer shorts, ties, bathrobes and more!

The American School of Needlework (ASN Publishing) is a great source for cross stitch design books, including one called *The Ultimate Cross Stitch Alphabet Book*. If you don't want to stitch by hand, check out the amazing things you can create with an embroidery machine today!

Embellishing Your Expressions

Depending on the materials and style of your project you can also embellish expressions with raffia, jute, wire, paper twist, ribbons, lace, trims, buttons, charms, shells, fabric motifs, lace appliqués or miniature accessories. To add unique appeal to cloth dolls and animals use short expressions on mini signs or cut out wood shapes.

You are only limited by your imagination, so go on . . . get creative!

Expect Miracles

An angel's heart is filled with love.

We Believe in Angels

Angels can fly because they take themselves lightly

Earthly angels are

Mothers in disguise

Listening hearts hear angels sing

Angel Crossing

An angel's work is NEVER DONE

Angels sent from up above Please protect the ones we love

I ♥ Angels

Angels Gather Here

Angel Collector

ANGELS ON DUTY

An angel is... as an angel does

Never drive faster than angels can fly

When in doubt, look up!

Angels light the way

Bless This Home With Love

Life is precious
handle with prayer

Smile
God Loves You

Bless This Country Home

Lord,
Grant me the patience
to endure my blessings

Count your blessings
day by day
And all your cares
will fly away.

Thou Shalt Not Whine

May God Keep You
In His Care

May the dear lord bless
and keep me safe

Shalom Means Everything

When things look down... look up

GOD is LOVE
⇥ ♥ ⇤

Gods biggest treasures
are his little ones

Thank heaven for..
babies
little girls
little boys

BABY

9

Dear Santa:
I want it
ALL!
xox

Santa & Co. est. 1995

Joy To The World
We Believe

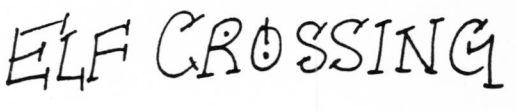
ELF CROSSING

Have a jingle *bright*
Christmas

SANTA
Stops
Here

Just say
Ho!

Twinkle, Twinkle
Christmas Star

Have a Heavenly Christmas

Sleigh
Parking

REINDEER
CROSSING

There's no people
like SNOWPEOPLE

All other vehicles
will be snowed!

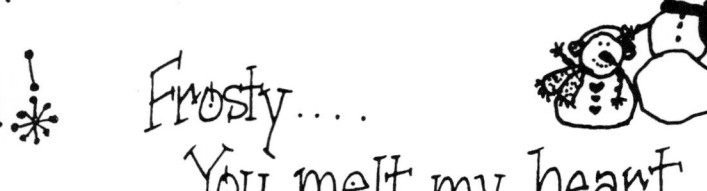
Frosty....
You melt my heart.

10

Jesus is the Reason for the Season

Peace Unto The World

Christ is the best part of Christmas

Let it snow . . . .
Let it snow . . . .
Let it snow . . . .

Make a joyful sound

Have Yourself a Merry Little Christmas

ELF*MADE

And to all a GOOD NIGHT

Just B___ Claus

May the Magic of Christmas Shine in Your Heart

We Believe in Santa

No HUMBUGS allowed.

• North Pole ↑
• Brake for Reindeer

Christmas is for Sharing & Caring

♥ ♥ *All Hearts Come Home For Christmas* ♥ ♥

Love Me
Love My Dog

The only self cleaning thing
in this Kitchen is
THE CAT....

Forget the dog
BEWARE of the KIDS!

ATTACK CAT
ON DUTY

Cutie
Cat

WIPE YOUR PAWS

From me-ow
To YOU

Blessed are the PURR in heart

Dogs think they are human
Cats know they are

We had to get rid of the kids
The cat was allergic.

You're purr...r...fect

Home Tweet Home

If you want the best seat
in the house
You'll have to move the cat

Every bird loves his own nest BEST!

Cat'cha
later.

 # Everybunny is Welcome

H O P
ON
IN

Somebunny Loves You

Wool Ewe Be Mine?

Ewe's Wooly Wonderful

Everyone Loves Somebunny

This bunny loves you !

Ewe are my sunshine

there's only one ewe

I LOVE YOU
MOO AND MOO
EACH DAY

Home is where your herd is

Waddle I do without you?

What's Moo with Ewe?

Udder chaos lives here.

Love one an-udder

It's ewe and me
FOREVER

Beware of Stampedes

EWE ARE LOVED

Doll Collector
at Heart

one can never have too many dolls

Never too old to play with dolls! ♥

Doll Crossing

Some of my best friends are......
DOLLS

Dolly's blue....
without you.

I'm just a Raggedy Ann
in a Barbie Doll World.

Discover your inner child —
Play with dolls! ♥

The nicest dreams
that will ever be...
are the dreams shared
by my dolly and me.

Dolls are like potato chips........
You can't have just one.

I can hardly wait till night time falls
when I crawl into bed with my favorite dolls

The Best Place To Be Is In A Loving Family

We can handle any problem
We have kids

The best thing to
Spend on your children
is
TIME

Our---family
is-a-circle-of-love

Childhood is a
journey.....
not a race.

Children are like seeds.....
Nurture them with love.

Sisters by fate,
Friends by choice.

Mothers of little boys
Work from SON up
til SON down.

Always my sister
forever my friend

There's no better
friend......
than a brother

Families are Forever

Babies are made in heaven.

Babies add so much love to life

Babies are ......
a miracle of LOVE

Babies are a treasure from above.

A mother holds her children's hands
for a little while...
and their hearts forever

A mother's love grows
FOREVER

"A mother's love is like a melody"

God made you my MOM
Love made you my FRIEND!

A mother's love
is tied with
heartstrings

Dad's the Boss

Mom said

shhh....Dad's Sawing Logs

To our children
We can give two things
One is roots
The other is wings.

Anyone can be a father
but it takes someone
special to be a Daddy

16

Our Most Treasured Family Heirlooms
Are Our Sweet Family Memories

There's no place like home........ except Grandma's

Grandpas are just antique little boys

Grandmas are..... just antique little girls

Grandpa's Fixin' Shop

A Grandma is a treasure of memories

If Mom says NO! call 1♥800♥GRANDMA

Grandma's Kitchen KIDS EAT FREE!

Nana means love.

Grandmas are for hugs & cookies XOX

Nana's the name — spoiling is the game.

A Family Stitched Together with love...... Seldom unravells.

17

A good friend is one
who comes in
when the whole world
goes out

Between the houses of friends, the road is never long

Family and friends
make a house
a home.

A friend listens
with the heart.

Old Friends Make the Best Antiques

Friendship is a Work of Heart

Friends are flowers that never fade.

Plant seeds of trust row on row...
And you will see a friendship grow.

*The seasons may come and go
but friends last forever*

Friendship is a treasure......
with a value beyond measure.

Friends are hugs for the heart

Back door friends are
always best.

Friends Become Chosen Family

Friends know the art
of giving from
the Heart

Friends see
Heart to Heart

18

When friends meet
♡ hearts warm. ♡

FRIENDSHIP IS A
RAINBOW
BETWEEN
TWO PEOPLE

Good friends
are
4 KEEPS

A friend is a very special blessing

Friendship is for
caring and sharing

Rain or shine,
You're a friend
of mine...

Neighbours are side by side
FRIENDS

Nothing Warms the Heart Like a Friend

Friends are flowers
in life's garden.

Pick your friends
but not to pieces.

Friendship is the thread in the patchwork of life.

*You have to be a good friend ...
to have one*

Friends are always at home
♥ ♥ in our hearts ♥ ♥ ♥

*Good Times & Friends Dear
Forever Welcome Here*

A FRIEND IS
A FOREVER THING

Laughter Prolongs Life

Life is full of
UPS & POUNDS!

Dieting is wishful shrinking.

Never eat more than you can lift

I'm not FAT.... I'm FLUFFY!

Spend til the end! $

A woman's place
is in the mall.

$

When the going gets tough,
The tough go shopping

Menopausal Maniac

I am man
Hear me ROAR
(while I snore.)

Bald is another word for "combing impaired."

Marriages are made in heaven...
so is thunder and lightning

If Friends Were Noses,
I'd Pick You

I can't be out of money
I still have checks left
(cheques)

20

Too Much of a Good Thing is Wonderful

Keep your temper—
no one else wants it.

Never go to bed MAD....
Stay up and fight.

YOU'RE ONE IN A MELON

Blondes Prefer Gentlemen

Money isn't everything.....
But it sure keeps the kids
in touch.

Give me patience.......
but please hurry.

**It's easier to hear a secret
than to keep one**

A closed mouth ......
gathers no feet.

I'll stop procrastinating......
TOMORROW

If it weren't for the
last minute.....
nothing would get done.

**Of all the things I've lost...
I miss my mind the most**

Garden Sweet Garden

GARDEN of WEEDIN'

Cultivate a Gratitude Attitude.

BLOOM where you're planted.

Gardening......
just another day
at the plant...

Earth Laughs In Flowers

Gardeners spread
THE BEST DIRT!

Free Weeds
U-PICK

I carrot about you!

If friends were carrots . . .
I would pick you

Scatter seeds of kindness
.....wherever you go.......

BEWARE
of SNAP DRAGONS

In my garden love grows

Welcome to our Patch

Plant Kindness
& Gather Some Love

Mom's Garden
Dad's Weeds

How does your garden grow?

MIND YOUR MUMMY

**BEST WITCHES
&
HAPPY HAUNTING**

Broom Parking 5¢

Have a spooktacular Halloween !

Forget the ghosts,
Beware of the sugar bugs

BLOOD DONORS NEEDED
SEE THE COUNT

BROOMS 4 SALE
Flying Lessons 10¢

BAT MOM

HOME OF THE WICKED WITCH
AND ALL HER LITTLE MONSTERS

Off we go a-haunting

Hoppy Easter

♡ You are eggstra special ♡

You're egg...cellent !

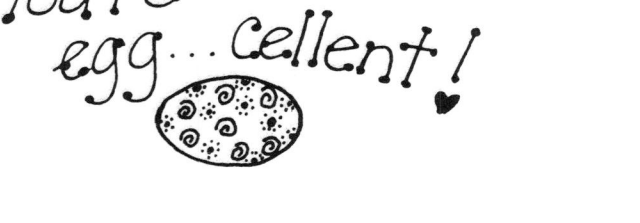

♥ You're no bunny 'til somebunny loves you. ♥♥

23

No Smoking - Country Air

If you smoke – leave your butt outside!

How Wonderful . . .
the little things in life can be

Don't Smoke -
You might Croak!

People with time for others
are happy around the clock.

Peace
is not a season
it's a way of life

It's a small world.........
let's live together in peace.

Life by the yard
is hard
By the inch...
a cinch.

Fertilize Yourself
take your vitamins

EXPERIENCE IS THE BEST TEACHER......
but the tuition is costly.

Good Planets are hard to find

ATTENTION:
We Interrupt This Marriage for Craft Show Season

Behind every creative person
is a closet full of ideas

Just say "No" to ~~crafts~~ housework.

**I Know You Can Make It,
But Will You?**

I only craft on days
that end with "y"

Creative clutter
is better than
idle neatness

You can always count on
X - Stitchers

Music gives the
... wings.

CRAFTS FOREVER,
HOUSEWORK WHENEVER

I'm creative
You can't expect me
to be neat too!

I'm not unorganized,
I just need a bigger Craft Room

25

Together is a wonderful place to be.

There's no place like home.

No matter what,
no matter where,
it's always home
if love is there

Home is where
you hang your

Happiness is homemade.

Love is homespun.

Home is where
your ♥ is.

East or West
Home is best.

A house is made of wood and stone
but only love can make it a home

Enter with a happy heart.

Welcome to Grand Central Station.

Joy to all who enter here

Back door friends are always best.

Welcome to our nest

Bachelor Pad
Enter at Your Own Risk

Home Tweet Home

A man's home is his castle...
until the queen arrives

A happy home is where both mates
think they got better than they deserve

Here may you live
Life at its best
May you find
Comfort and rest

Love is so nice
to come home to.

Good Food ♥ Good Friends ♥ Good Times

Bless those who clean up

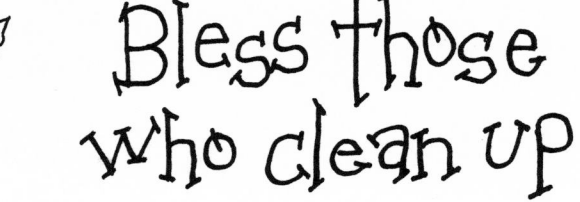

This house is protected by killer dust bunnies

Four Letter Dirty Words

Wash, Cook, Iron & Dust

Dust is a protective cover for furniture

"M" is for Mother not - Maid

HOME SWEET PAD

HOUSEWORK MAKES ME WANT TO CROAK!

Housework makes you homely.

Dull women have immaculate houses.

HELP WANTED: Everyone in this house qualified.

Too much housework can cause brain damage

28

Bless This Mess

HOUSEWORK STINKS

BATHROOM RULES
Wash
Brush
Floss
&
Flush

Dust is just
a country accent.

♡ Cross my country heart ♡

HOUSE RULES:
1. Mom's the Boss
2. See Rule #1.

I clean house every other day —
this is not the other day

Where are all the spoons?
With all the lost socks.

Is there life
after
laundry?

If you write in the dust.... please don't date it.

My house is clean enough to be healthy
Dirty enough to be happy

A woman's work is never done —
because she's never home

29

Plant goals
& harvest dreams

THOSE WHO
REACH
TOUCH THE STARS

Aim for your star

Wish upon a star

Look for life's greatest treasures
in life's simplest pleasures.

Enjoy The Journey

Believe to achieve

Paint your own rainbows
in LiFE.

Believe in Yourself

Try to fix the problem....
...not the blame

The city of happiness is in the state of mind.

Ideas never work ...
unless we do

A happy memory is a forever joy.

Most worries are reruns.

The best way to be special....
is to be yourself.

30

Dare to be different

♥ LIVE WELL ♥ LAUGH OFTEN ♥ LOVE MUCH ♥

PRACTICE
MAKES
PERFECT

Commit random acts of kindness
and senseless acts of beauty.

Happy is ye thankful heart

Put your heart in it

Dreams are a wish
your heart makes.

The most important things in life...
aren't things

For every problem there is
an opportunity.

Make stepping stones out of stumbling stones

Be an original.....
not a copy.

March to your own drummer.

It's not how much you have.
It's how you enjoy it.

If you must, you can

31

If there seems to be
no bright side in your life....
polish up your dark side.

The gift of happiness belongs to those who unwrap it.

DARE TO DREAM

A smile
adds a great deal
to one's face value

Time is nature's way of
preventing everything
from happening
at once.

STOP
to
smell the
flowers

SMILE
it's catching

Think BIG

The best preparation for tomorrow . . .
is the best use of today

Share the warmth
♥ of your smile ♥

FOLLOW YOUR DREAMS

Save yourself a lot of trouble.
Don't borrow any.

You're never
fully dressed
til you wear a SMILE!

My Kitchen and Me Welcome Thee

Complaints to the cook
can be hazardous to your health.

KISS THE COOK

I made my favorite thing for dinner . . .
a reservation

Just say **No!**
to cooking.

A Messy Kitchen is a Happy Place
This One is DELIRIOUS!

In the cookie of life,
FRIENDS are the chocolate chips.

No matter where
I serve my guests,
they seem to like
my kitchen best

Season Everything
With Love

This is a self cleaning kitchen
Everyone cleans up after themselves.

Keep this Kitchen clean....
EAT OUT

I don't do mornings.

Is it coffee yet?

This kitchen is
SELFSERVE

33

Be kind......
Feelings are everywhere.

Love lives in happy hearts

Love

Love is a present
We can give.
every single day.

Life is for Living
Love is for Giving.

Love is Homespun

Letters mingle the souls.

This gift is all wrapped and tied,
With wishes of love all tucked inside....

Love is the glue that
holds the world together.

Let all that you do
be done in love.

Miles can't separate
hearts that care

The best gifts are tied
with heartstrings

All things grow with love

Love doesn't make
the world go round
...but it sure makes
the ride worthwhile.

Joy shared
is joy doubled.

Love is love reflected

If thoughts of you made stars appear
new galaxies would unfold here

Many can teach,
only a special few can reach

Computer Wizard!

Teachers plant the seeds of the future

Doctors have a lot of PATIENTS....

Teachers have CLASS

To err is human,
but it's against company policy

Teaching is to touch a life forever.

I've used up all my sick days....
Now I'm calling in dead.....

 A+ teacher

 Teaching is a work of heart

To err is human but..
to really foul things up
requires a computer

If you can read this — thank a teacher!

 Teaching is the profession....
that creates all others.

Teachers make a difference.

Accountants are well balanced people.

Teachers Touch the Future

Old accountants never die,
they just lose their figures.

Be nice to your children, for they will choose your rest home *Over the hill*

I'm not aging.....
I'm marinating.

It's not a matter of growing old,
It's getting old if you stop growing

Over the hill . . . and picking up speed.

**Young at heart,
slightly older in other places**

NATURAL AGING WOMAN

You're only young once.
But you can be immature.
FOREVER

*Wrinkles are not so bad, they just show
where smiles have been*

Age doesn't matter...
unless your chesse

After 40 —
it's a matter of maintenance.

The older the violin
The sweeter the music

**I'm not young enough
to know everything**

BETTER TO BE OVER THE HILL . . . . .
THAN UNDER IT !

Tennis is my racket

We interrupt
this marriage
for { hockey or
golf or
baseball
season.

Old skiers never die
they just go downhill

Old soccer players never die
they just lose their kick!

Tall fish tales
told here

Golf Stories Told Here
(slightly exaggerated)

Gone fishin'
Just for the halibut

I golf...
therefore I lie

I'm hooked on fishin'

When I die throw me in a lake
so my husband will fish for ME!

Golf is a steady
diet of greens

Good things come
to those who bait

Life is a game
but golf is serious!

Old fishermen never die,
they just smell that way

37

A quilt is something you make
To keep someone you love.....
WARM.

Anytime is stitchin time

A quilt is a blanket of Love

Sewing and Crafts
fill my days
not to mention
the livingroom, bedroom
and closets.

Touch these scissors
and die!

Memories are stitched
With love.

My Soul Is Fed
By Needle & Thread

Good friends are like quilts,
They never lose their warmth

In the crazy quilt of life,
I'm glad you're in
my block of friends.

I'm in therapy &
SEWING is cheaper
than a psychiatrist.

Quilts are like friends—
a great source of comfort.

Sew much fabric
So little time.

Behind every sewer
is a huge pile
of fabric.

Quilters never
cut corners

You're SEW SPECIAL

♥ From my hands..... To your heart ♥ ♥ ♥

Buttons and patches and the cold wind blowing The days pass quickly When I am sewing! ♥

When life gives you scraps... make quilts.

She who dies with the most fabric..... WINS!

Love is the thread that binds us

Anytime is stitchin time

friendships are sewn.... one stitch at a time.....

A Family Stitched Together With Love . . .
Seldom Unravells

A family is a patchwork of LOVE

Quilting with a friend Will keep you in stitches.

Blessed are the.... Piecemakers!

Quilters never grow old, They just go to pieces.

Life is a patchwork of FRIENDS

I ♥ SEWING and HAVE PLENTY of MATERIAL WITNESSES

Love makes all things BEARABLE!

Teddy bears are stuffed with dreams and memories

♥♥ Love breeds teddy bears
Teddy bears breed love ♥♥

WANTED: child to love. Age 1 to 101

Beauty is in the eyes of the "bear" holder

Love me......
Love my teddy bear.

YOU'RE BEARY SPECIAL

♡ Nothing satisfies like a good bear hug ♡

Beary Best Friends

Sometimes love is a little heart to bear ★

Aa Bb Cc Dd Ee Ff

Gg Hh Ii Jj Kk Ll

Mm Nn Oo Pp Qq Rr

Ss Tt Uu Vv Ww Xx

Yy Zz

1 2 3 4 5 6 7 8 9 0

Aa Bb Cc Dd Ee Ff

Gg Hh Ii Jj Kk Ll

Mm Nn Oo Pp Qq Rr

Ss Tt Uu Vv Ww Xx

Yy Zz.

1 2 3 4 5 6 7 8 9 0

Aa Bb Cc Dd
Ee Ff Gg Hh
Ii Jj Kk Ll
Mm Nn Oo
Pp Qq Rr Ss
Tt Uu Vv
Ww Xx Yy
Zz 0 1 2 3 4 5
6 7 8 9

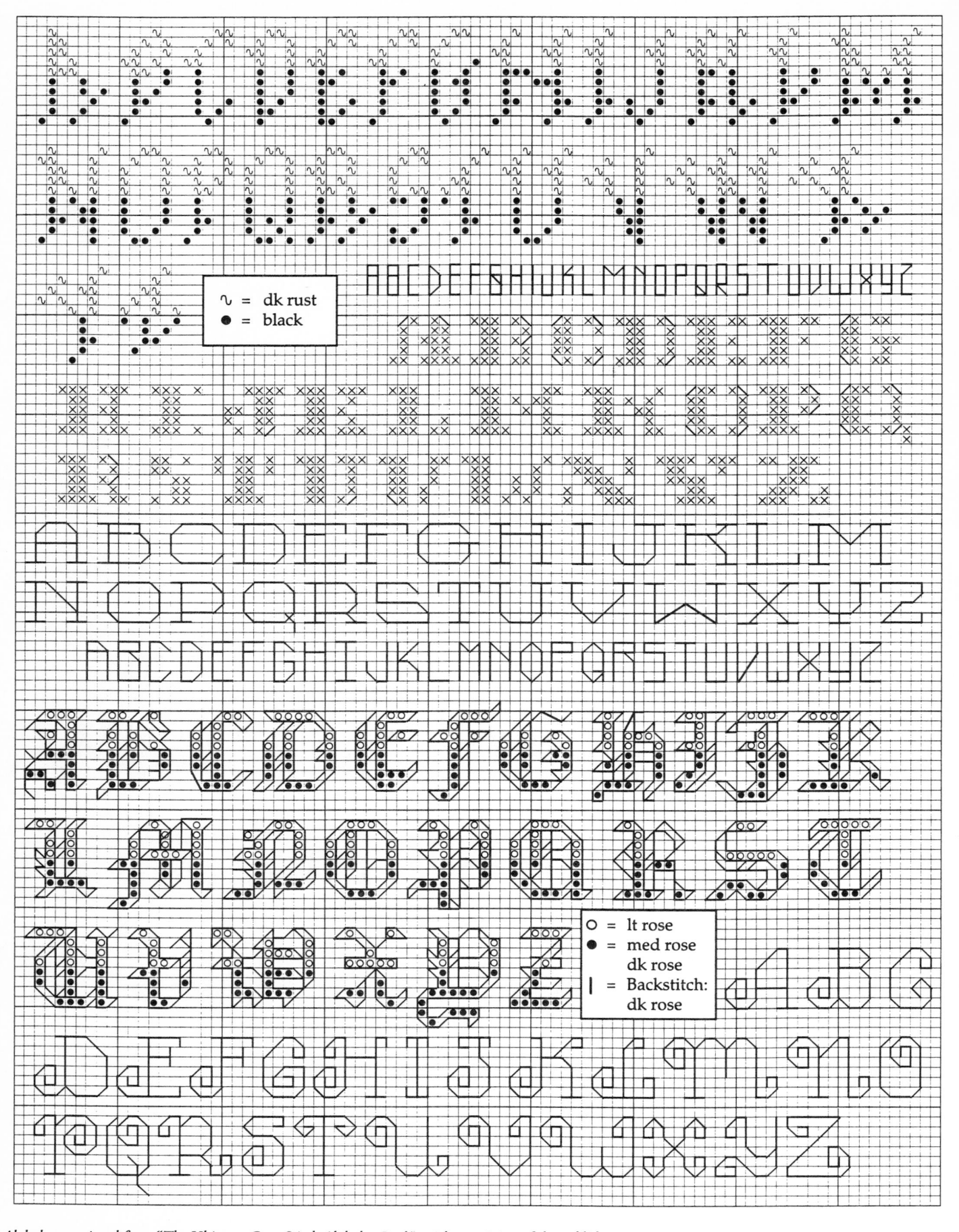

Alphabets reprinted from "The Ultimate Cross Stitch Alphabet Book", with permission of the publisher,
American School of Needlework® Inc., ©1992, Kooler Design Studio Inc.